Teens and Divorce

Look for these and other books in the Lucent
Overview Series:

Teen Alcoholism
Teen Depression
Teen Dropouts
Teen Drug Abuse
Teen Eating Disorders
Teen Parenting
Teen Pregnancy
Teen Prostitution
Teens and Divorce
Teens and Drunk Driving
Teen Sexuality
Teen Smoking
Teen Suicide
Teen Violence

Teens and Divorce

by Gail B. Stewart

TEEN ISSUES

LUCENT Overview Series

LUCENT *Overview Series*

Library of Congress Cataloging-in-Publication Data

Stewart, Gail, 1949–
    Teens and divorce / by Gail B. Stewart.
        p.   cm. — (Lucent overview series. Teen issues)
    Includes bibliographical references and index.
    ISBN 1-56006-656-3   (lib.: alk. paper)
        1. Divorce—Juvenile literature. 2. Broken homes—Juvenile
    literature. 3. Children of divorced parents—Juvenile literature.
    4. Parent and teenager—Juvenile literature.   I. Title.   II. Series.
    HQ814.S7935   2000
    306.89—dc21   99-046614

Copyright © 2000 by Lucent Books, Inc.
P.O. Box 289011, San Diego, CA 92198-9011
Printed in the U.S.A.

Contents

Introduction

IN 1961, WHEN SHE was thirteen, Barbara's parents divorced. Divorce was far from being a commonplace occurrence then—in fact, Barbara remembers that she was the only one in her grade who lived in a one-parent household. "Back then, in the town I lived in, the dads went off to work and the moms stayed home," she says. "But after the divorce, my mom was working at the dry cleaner's. I remember feeling so sad; I felt so different from all the other kids.

"My mom wasn't around when my sister and I got home from school. She couldn't do things at our school like she had in the past—help with my sister's Halloween party, things like that. I remember thinking that it was like my family had this horrible secret that we couldn't talk about, and that made everything worse."[1]

A last resort

Barbara's sense of being different was an accurate feeling in the 1960s since divorce was not at all common then. Psychologists who deal with family issues explain that in that era, marriage was more commonly considered an unbreakable institution—especially if there were children involved. There was the idea, explains one expert, "that parents have a duty and an obligation—to their children, to each other, and to the larger society—to place their children's needs above their own individual interests."[2]

Some marriages did end in divorce, but usually only as a last resort, appropriate only in the most extreme cases of marital difficulty. It was believed that parents could work out most problems in their marriage more easily than children could handle the difficulties that would come from their parents' divorcing.

"If a husband was beating his wife, then divorce was looked at as appropriate," says one counselor. "Or if one partner abandoned the family—then sure. But people didn't get divorced because of reasons such as 'We're just growing apart' or 'We have different interests' like they do today. Back then, maintaining the marriage—almost at all costs—was absolutely the aim."[3]

Changing attitudes

But attitudes about marriage and divorce began to change very quickly after 1960. One clear indicator of this was a survey conducted by the *Journal of Marriage and the Family*. Women were asked if they disagreed with the statement: "When there are children in the family, parents should stay together even if they don't get along." The survey in 1962 showed that about 51 percent of women disagreed; however, by 1977 the same question posed to the same sample of women found 80 percent disagreeing. Within fifteen years, notes one psychologist, "this group of women had moved from divided opinion to an overwhelming consensus that unhappily married parents should not stay together for the children's sake."[4]

The statistics on divorce since 1960 certainly reflect this change in opinion. After the early 1960s, the rate of divorce in the United States ballooned—doubling in less than a decade between 1963 and 1972. In 1995 more than 16.2 million Americans were divorced. It is estimated that just over half of marriages in 1999 will end in divorce.

Children in the mix

Such statistics are disturbing because they show that many couples are experiencing emotional distress and unhappiness in their marriages. Far more disturbing, say adolescent psychologists, are the millions of young people who are innocent bystanders in divorce, the victims caught in the middle of their parents' deteriorating relationship.

U. S. Divorce Rates		
Year	**Divorce Rate** (among total population)	**Divorce Rate** (among women 15 and older)
1940	2.0%	8.8%
1946	4.3%	17.9%
1951	2.5%	9.9%
1957	2.2%	9.2%
1965	2.5%	10.6%
1970	3.5%	14.9%
1975	4.8%	20.3%
1979	5.3%	22.8%
1981	5.3%	22.6%
1985	5.0%	21.7%
1990	4.7%	20.9%
1993	4.6%	20.5%
1994	4.6%	20.5%

Source: National Center for Health Statistics.

Experts know that in many ways, divorce is harder on teens and younger children than on the parents themselves. While parents may feel that the divorce is a solution to their problems—even a new beginning—the child's perspective is almost always more negative. There is anger at the parents, as well as grief for the way of life that can't continue. Except for the death of a parent, say counselors, there is nothing more devastating to an adolescent.

The numbers of youth who are experiencing that devastation grow every year. Each day in the United States, three thousand young people become children of divorce. But just because a large number of teens find themselves in a family that is dissolving, it doesn't mean that divorce is any less painful, especially for the individuals involved.

Although the divorce itself is often a relatively simple legal matter, the flurry of feelings and changes experienced by the children of divorcing parents is far more involved, far more complex. For teens, at the stage in life in which they are trying to establish their own place in the world, the added element of their parents' divorce can be especially traumatic. The experience often makes them question ideas they have about love and commitment, about marriage and family.

"To say that divorce is a scary time for teens is a real understatement," says one expert. "But that isn't to say that they can't get through the changes, the upheavals—they can. But it's *how* they get beyond those things, how they deal with it all and come out on the other side intact—that's the challenge that's going to determine what kind of adults those kids will become."[5]

1

Cracks in the Foundation

THE IDEA OF divorce is frightening to a teen for a variety of reasons. Divorce may mean having to move to a new home in a new neighborhood—even a new city. A teenage child of divorcing parents may have to face another kind of separation: leaving one school and friends behind and starting over in a new school.

There are frequently changes in the family finances, especially if one parent is dependent on the other's child support payments. A mother who worked part-time before the divorce might be forced to work full-time to make ends meet. When that happens, the teen may face more responsibilities at home, such as helping with meals or watching a younger brother or sister.

These are changes that may occur *later*, after the parents have made the decision to divorce. But experts are quick to point out that divorce is a process, and there are changes within the family early on, even before the parents separate. Arguing and fighting between parents can create an atmosphere that is not only tense, but confusing—not only to younger children, but to teens as well.

Everybody fights

Every marriage has conflict; any relationship has times when there is unhappiness or tension that sometimes boils to the surface for everyone in the family to see. People change, and as they change they sometimes rethink various aspects of their lives. Regardless of their ages, when they notice conflict children may worry that their parents are planning a divorce. But of course, arguing and fighting—even on a frequent basis—are not necessarily signals that parents are going to divorce.

Therese stayed home with her children when they were small, but once they were all in school, she took a job outside the home as a nurse. Her husband, she says, was not as pleased with the new arrangement as she was. "It was different," she admits. "There were two nights each week when Bill came home before I did, and he had to get the kids from the sitter and start dinner. It wasn't what he was used to—I'd always had supper on the table when he came in at 5:45, but that just wasn't happening every night.

"It was hard on me, too—I missed out on some things in the evening that I enjoyed. Some of Justin's soccer games, things like that. But the extra money helped, and Bill was glad for that. But we had lots of arguments about it. He was tired and so was I—just a change in the relationship, I guess. But it worked out, because we were determined that it would."[6]

Growing in different directions

Many couples find themselves in the same position as Therese and Bill; they have conflicts occasionally and deal with them. Sometimes this can mean arguments and friction, but in the end, through hard work and effort, the conflicts are resolved.

But there are other couples who don't seem to be able to resolve their conflicts, despite plenty of hard work. In some cases, they argue over the same things time after time, without making any progress in resolving their differences. Sometimes the differences themselves have no solutions.

"Sometimes it's just a matter of people being in a completely different place than they were when they fell in love," says one counselor. "Perhaps they married young and as they grew up, they grew apart, with different interests and ideas. Sometimes financial hardships cause

*Overhearing parents'
frequent arguments can
be frightening to chil-
dren, who often believe
the fighting will lead to
divorce.*

problems between them. Or perhaps one of them has met
someone else who fits his or her life much better.

"Whatever the reason—and there are many—these couples don't value the relationship as they once did. And
when love is no longer there, there isn't as much of a reason to put in the effort fixing what's not working."[7]

When the fighting seems to resolve nothing and the will
to find solutions is absent, the atmosphere at home often

gets more and more tense. That tension is felt by everyone present. No matter how old the children of a fighting couple are, the arguing takes a toll on them.

"Our family would never be the same"

Children who witness relentless arguments experience a number of worries. They might be concerned with the loudness of the voices, or crying—especially if they have never before seen their parents in such emotional states.

Shana, sixteen, recalls how it made her feel when she came home early from a friend's house after school and found her parents in the middle of an emotionally charged argument. "They weren't exactly yelling at each other," she remembers. "It was more like crying and stuff. I'd never seen my parents cry before—I mean, I'd seen my mom get teary-eyed sometimes, like at my sister's graduation. But my dad—never! And here they both were, really crying.

"I can't describe it exactly—it was sort of like I wanted to erase the whole thing from my mind. But every time I closed my eyes, for like months afterward, I'd think of that."[8]

Other reactions

Sometimes teens feel embarrassed about their parents' arguments, especially if there is a lot of yelling. They may be nervous about the cause of the fighting, especially if they themselves were mentioned by their arguing parents. But the most common worry, say teens, is that their parents will divorce and thereby destroy the family forever.

Shawn, a thirteen-year-old whose parents are divorced, knows this firsthand. "That was the thing that was the hardest to think about," he admits. "I mean, my mom and dad had some really bad fights before they split up—and my mom would tell me that the yelling would stop when my dad moved out.

"But it was just the idea of him leaving that was weird. I didn't like their fighting any more than my brothers did, but in a way, I'd rather have them together and fighting than think about our whole family breaking apart. It just felt wrong that our family would never be the same, ever again."[9]

Psychologists say that Shawn's feelings are very normal, since of all the parts of a young person's life, the family is the foundation—the solid rock upon which everything else rests. "Friends come and go, parents' jobs change, the family moves," says therapist Lynn Kiely. "And though all of these things may cause some turmoil for a teen, they don't usually cause too much trauma as long as the family is intact. The family structure is the bedrock—it's the constant in life."[10]

The need for consistency

Although teens sometimes seem aloof and uninterested in family matters, experts contend that they are still deeply affected by parental conflicts.

Ironically, however, many parents are convinced that their teenage children are no longer interested enough in the family to know when there are problems. On the contrary, they say, their teenage children seem to be so wrapped up in themselves and their friends that family life seems a low priority. "If I went by how often my daughters [ages thirteen and fourteen] actually speak to me to gauge

my importance in their lives," says one mother, rolling her eyes, "I'd rank myself down there with homework and tetanus shots. They spend more time on the phone with their friends than talking with me. If I mention that we're all doing a 'family thing' some Sunday afternoon, they shriek and wail.

"On the occasions when we do have a conversation, it seems like it goes badly—either I say something to annoy one of them, or vice versa. If I didn't know better, I guess I'd assume my absence would be more of a relief to my girls. But I've been there—I remember what it feels like to be that age, so I remind myself that I can't take any of this personally. It will pass!" [11]

A normal part of growing up

Interestingly, many parents in past decades took this passing attitude toward family for true indifference on the part of teens. Some well-meaning counselors used to advise warring parents to wait until their young children were in high school before going through with a divorce, since the change wouldn't upset them as much then.

Experts now say that contrary to how teens act, the family and its well-being are exceedingly important to them. At the same time, it is very true that teens are at a point in their lives where their need for independence—especially from parents and teachers—seems to outweigh reliance. Whereas a few years earlier they would have gone to a parent about a problem or worry, they instead talk to their friends. They often feel their parents' involvement in their lives is an intrusion.

While this breaking away from parents and family is a normal part of development, it is often a painful time for parents. "For most parents, the teen years mark the first time since their child's birth that they don't feel needed," explains child development expert Gary Neuman. "Compared to younger children, teenagers seem to want much less of our time, our advice, and our companionship. . . . [P]arents can feel they've been displaced, and in a sense they have, at least temporarily." [12]

"Don't you guys know you're scaring me?"

But as aloof and disinterested as teens might seem toward their parents, friction between a mother and father can be very unsettling. A teen who comes home from school to find his or her parents red-eyed and angry can't help but worry. One seventeen-year-old boy whose parents separated eight months ago admits that he had been nervous for years that his parents' fighting meant they were headed for divorce. "They screamed at each other all the time over stupid, unimportant things like where were the car keys," he remembers. "It just seemed like every day there was something really insignificant that they fought about. I remember when I was nine or so, I just panicked when they fought, especially at night.

"I'd lie in bed and listen to them, and try really hard to think positive thoughts, like I could affect what they were saying. I think I figured that if I willed them to lower their voices or to laugh, then everything would be all right. I wanted to yell at them, 'Don't you guys know you're scaring me?' But of course, you can't do something like that when you're nine." [13]

More than yelling

In some households, the quarreling becomes even uglier and more frightening when there is physical violence involved. One fourteen-year-old boy remembers his father hitting his mother with a broom handle when she spent too much money on groceries—even though, he says, she never bought anything that expensive. "It's not like we were eating steak or lobster," he explains. "My mom would come home with the bags, and he'd just start going off on her. Her legs and arms would get all black and blue, and she wouldn't want to go to her job for a few days.

"She told me that he had anger problems, and that he didn't mean the things he said to her. I didn't care about his problems, I was just glad when she got a divorce. She ended up getting a restraining order so he couldn't come near us, and I'm glad. I guess for me, it wasn't too bad that my parents got divorced. I'm glad, really—I think it probably saved my mom's life."[14]

"Love is supposed to be this big deal, this thing that lasts forever"

The notion of one's parents splitting up is frightening enough, but there is the other fear of what will happen to teens when their mother or father leaves. Will they have to leave their school and friends? An uncertain future is often more terrifying than the unpleasant situation in which a teen is now living.

"It was hard for me because my parents didn't really have time to really talk to us," says one sixteen-year-old.

In some households, escalating arguments lead to physical violence.

"They were so busy hurting each other, calling each other names, and making sure they had the last word, they sort of forgot about my brother and me.

"Back then, both of us were worried about what was going to happen, yeah. I mean, the way my mom and dad talked, it didn't seem like Todd and I were exactly a priority for them. Todd's three years younger than me, and I know he was more scared than I was. He'd say stuff to me like, 'Do you think we'll end up in a foster home?' or 'What if both of them leave?' He was really scared about that, and I guess I was, too." [15]

Counselors say the idea that a married couple could stop loving one another is a frightening one. Children—even older teens—can't help but wonder about the nature of love, and this is a major worry of teens. After all, if their parents stop loving one another, is it possible that they could stop loving their children, too?

"Love is supposed to be this big deal, this thing that lasts forever," says Sheila, thirteen. "I'm not a little baby, and I know things happen. But in all the movies, all the books, when you fall in love, that's it. It's supposed to be a commitment, something sacred. And then your mom says she doesn't love your dad anymore. I mean, what's that about? How can love just stop?" [16]

Needing to be at home

Even when parents try to keep their arguments private, however, the tension that exists in a house where the parents are always fighting can have a variety of effects on their children. Some teens say that life at home with quarreling parents is like living in the middle of a battlefield and admit they feel frightened and apprehensive a lot of the time.

Sixteen-year-old Ben's parents divorced three years ago. In the months before they split up, he felt that he needed to spend more time at home, because he feared what would happen when he was gone. "I'd worry that my dad would hurt my mom," he says. "I felt kind of like, 'Well, they'd have to be OK if I was around—they couldn't let things get too bad with their son right there in the house.' I know

Source: National Center for Health Statistics and U.S. Census Bureau.

U.S. Marriages and Divorces

	1990	1997
Marriage Statistics		
Marriages Annually	2,443,000	2,384,000
Marriage Rate (per 1,000 population)	9.8	8.9
Divorce Statistics		
Divorces Annually	1,182,000	1,163,000
Divorce Rate (per 1,000 population)	4.7	4.3

Likelihood of new marriages ending in divorce (1988): 43%

Percentage of general adult population (1998)

Current number of divorced adults: 19,400,000 — 9.8%

Current number of married adults living with spouse: 110,600,000 — 56%

Other — 44.2%

that's wrong—I know it *now*, at least. But back then, it seemed like I was sort of protecting them if I was there."

Asked what effect that had on his own life, Ben smiles. "I sort of turned into a hermit in eighth grade," he says. "My friends were always calling to do things, but I'd make up excuses, like I was sick or my parents and I were going out. I guess they wondered what was going on, but I didn't want to talk about it." [17]

Another teen also felt the need to stay home more often, but not out of any fear for the safety of her parents. She knew that her parents didn't argue as much when she and her younger sisters were at home and reasoned that their presence in the house would therefore keep arguments from occurring. "It was naive—I know that now," she says. "But at the time it seemed really smart. It was a real difference in lifestyle for me, because when I was little, I'd always be going to sleepovers at my friends' houses—no big deal. But I started staying around every weekend. I'd tell my friends I was busy, or any excuse.

"If anything, it might have made their arguments quieter. It didn't stop them, though. They still got divorced and it became really clear that there was nothing I could do to stop it, or prevent it, or anything." [18]

"No one wanted to be there"

Some teens have an opposite reaction. They find the constant bickering stressful and feel the need to stay away from home as much as possible. They go to friends' houses to spend the night more often or work longer hours at after-school jobs than before.

Katherine, seventeen, recalls that most of her childhood was spent running around in the swampy area behind her house—not, she says, because she was so outdoorsy, but rather because she was fleeing an unpleasant situation at home. "I mean, I liked [the outdoors], but I wasn't obsessed with it or anything," she explains. "I just liked being away from the house because my parents fought all the time. . . . No one wanted to be there. . . . I mean, my parents hated each other. If they hadn't gotten a divorce when they did, they probably would have ended up killing each other." [19]

"It's all my fault"

Another common reaction to parents' fighting is guilt. Younger children often feel that their parents' divorce is something that happened because they were naughty. And while a teen would laugh off such an idea, many teens worry that the arguing they hear is about them, about something they have or haven't done. Guilt is something a large majority of children—including teens—feel about parental fighting.

"It's the most common thing in the world," says one counselor. "Kids hear one parent being critical of the other's parenting methods, and the shouting takes on a whole new meaning, a more personal one. All of a sudden the problem isn't just between the mom and the dad, it's about the teenager himself.

"I had one boy tell me, 'Don't tell me my parents' divorce isn't about me! It's all my fault. I heard my dad yell at my mom because she bought me expensive basketball shoes—he was really upset. They fought all night because of that.' So to that boy, it all translated as 'If I hadn't asked for the shoes, my mom wouldn't have bought them and this fight wouldn't be happening.'"[20]

However, experts stress that children of divorcing parents should never feel responsible for their parents' fighting. The fact is that children and how to raise them is just one of the topics parents frequently fight about. Children

Most teens feel some level of guilt about their parents' arguments, especially when they hear parents disputing over child rearing issues.

do not have the power to keep an unhappy marriage intact any more than they have the power to break up two adults committed to a marriage.

"Parents fight about their kids because that's just one of the topics parents have strong personal feelings about. They disagree on what is best for the children, whether it's on discipline, homework, or piano lessons, whatever. But it is never the kids' fault that the parents divorce," says a counselor flatly. "Never."[21]

"I couldn't think about three plus four squared"

One of the most predictable effects of family tension is a teen's lack of interest in schoolwork. Under the best of circumstances, it is difficult for many teens to concentrate on school as they try to budget their time between their studies, a social life, and possibly a part-time job. But with the stress of their parents fighting—or not speaking—many young people have trouble getting homework done at all.

Sarah, fifteen, found her grades plummeting from A's to D's during the time before her parents split up. "I couldn't focus on my work," she remembers. "I just kept wondering whether my dad still loved me. I thought maybe I wasn't smart or good enough for him, and that's why he left."[22]

Another teen observes that school seemed like a complete waste of time when there was something of such huge importance going on at home. "I couldn't think about three plus four squared when my parents were screaming at each other," she says. "My attitude was like, 'Screw school!' I'd cut class and not turn in papers on time."[23]

Counselors say that the situation is ironic, for at the time when teens need parental involvement the most, parents are often at their worst. The combination of distraction at home and problems at school can turn into a downward spiral. "Parents are often scrambling to keep their lives together, to deal with the fighting and unpleasantness. Some are trying to decide whether to take that final step toward divorce. And I know the news that their daughter is skipping class to go to the mall or that their son is failing

It is often difficult for teens to concentrate on schoolwork when their problems at home seem to be of a much greater magnitude.

geometry doesn't seem as crucial at that very moment. Under normal circumstances, they'd be there for the kids. But these aren't normal circumstances." [24]

Teens whose parents are close to divorce would be the first to agree. "Normal circumstances" seem far removed from life in their families. And the normality becomes more remote as parents move from the "thinking about it" stage to the actual separation—the breaking up of the family.

2

The Mechanics of Divorce

THE PROCESS OF divorce is not a quick one. The legal part of divorce begins when one or both parents take steps to end the marriage contract. Usually that means hiring a lawyer who assists them in filing a petition explaining why they want a divorce. This document also explains how they feel the family responsibilities of each parent should be divided. But by the time parents take that step, they have usually found a time to break the news to their children.

Breaking the news

Psychologists say that although announcing the end of the marriage is extremely difficult for parents, receiving that news is even harder for the children. Hearing that parents are divorcing, they say, is only slightly less traumatic for a child than the death of a parent, so it's important that the parents do it right. Unfortunately, this is a task that is sometimes mishandled.

"I've had kids tell me real horror stories about how they were told," says one counselor. "One boy remembers his father telling him on the way to school one morning, just before he was dropped off. Can you imagine how that boy felt all day, how he coped? Another teenager said that as his parents were breaking the news to him and his brother, the parents actually started arguing about whose fault the divorce was." [25]

Many teens who have been through the experience agree that while there is probably no good time to hear about their parents' divorce, they prefer a quiet setting, with both parents present. "My mom and dad tried hard to make it OK," says Ryan, sixteen. "We went out to the arboretum near my grandma's house and they told us there. No ringing phones or people coming to the door, I guess. They were more uncomfortable than I'd ever seen them, though.

"At least they were together. My friend at school told me that when he found out about his parents splitting up, his mom told him. His dad just left the house and called him like a week later. His mom just told him what a jerk his father was, and how they would be better off.

"As it was for me and my brother and sister, it was the worst moment of our lives. But I know I'm glad my parents talked to us at the same time, anyway."[26]

According to psychologists, receiving the news that one's parents are divorcing can be one of the most traumatic events in a teen's life.

"What did they think—
I was completely deaf?"

Even when parents are successful in hiding their arguments from younger children, teens are usually very quick to pick up on the tension. As a result, most teens say that their parents' announcement of divorce is hardly a surprise. In such cases, learning that a divorce is going to happen may actually come as a relief.

"It was sort of a funny situation," says one boy. "My dad told us that he and my mom had something to tell us all, and so we got together on a Saturday morning—me and my sisters and my parents. They got this real serious look; both of them looked like they were going to start crying.

"Anyway, they start telling us the usual stuff all parents must say, like, 'We don't love each other but we love you,' and that kind of thing. And I'm just amazed how they think this is news. I mean, what did they think—I was completely deaf? I've been listening to my dad yell and my mom slam doors and cry for like years! I wanted to say, 'Do you people really think this is a surprise? The truth is, I'd been waiting for that little talk for a long time. It was a relief when it finally came."[27]

"I remember feeling shocked"

But while teens might be aware of the tension between their parents and might even be expecting a divorce, many admit that the announcement still stunned them. "I remember feeling shocked when they told us," says Rachel, fifteen. "In some ways I knew it was coming. It was the general atmosphere—it was tense. But it was totally different actually hearing it from them and knowing it was going to happen! I didn't know anyone whose parents were divorced, and it was just weird to think my parents were."[28]

Tom, seventeen, agrees. "In the back of my mind I always expected them to get divorced, ever since I was a little kid. It just seemed like they didn't *like* each other, let alone love each other. But when they finally told me, after all those years, I was surprised, and kind of sad. I think I

Many couples separate before making the decision to go through with a divorce.

maybe thought they could just keep going, you know? Just keep being married, the way they were. But they couldn't, and that was that."[29]

The separation

When parents make the decision to proceed with a divorce, it is very common for them to separate first. Occasionally, if the circumstances permit, they might sleep in separate rooms and occupy different areas of the house. But most of the time, one parent moves out of the house as the divorce process gets under way.

The separation—though not the legal ending of the marriage—is the most traumatic part of the divorce for parents to explain to the children, say counselors. "Telling your kids that one of you is going to move out is one of the hardest things you will ever have to do as a parent," psychologist Mary Ann Shaw advises divorcing parents. "It's even more difficult than talking to them about sex. You are hurting, and you know this news is going to hurt them."[30]

The hurt that teens feel is no less than that which younger children feel, although they might react in different ways. While younger children might cry and demand reassurance, teens often become angry. Sometimes their anger is directed inappropriately at the parent who they feel caused the separation. One woman remembers her daughter screaming at her the day her husband left, even though the separation was his idea. "Michelle watched him load up the last of his computer stuff in boxes and carry it to the car," she says. "He drove off, and Michelle starts yelling at me, 'If you'd been nicer to Daddy, he wouldn't have left! It's all your fault!' I'll tell you, I thought that my husband telling me he'd been cheating on me hurt—but adding my daughter's anger to that, I was a basket case. I don't think I've ever felt so awful."[31]

Self-absorbed

The feelings teens have about problems in their parents' marriage are strong, even though, as mentioned previously, teens often act disinterested. The separation of their parents, which is a critical time for teens, is physical proof—more so even than the fighting and arguing—that this solid home is coming apart. It is what psychologist Anthony Wolf calls "the paradox of adolescence."

"They want and need a home that they can count on despite the fact that at any given moment they may despise that home and the parent or parents in it, or even run away from it. A divorce undermines all of that, disrupting the base of security they need in order to face all the issues of adolescence. It produces a *forced* independence and a *real* growing up that no teenager ever truly wants."[32]

Teens are at an age when they are basically self-absorbed. They view events around them in a different way than a younger sibling would, often seeing the divorce as a personal affront. "My four-year-old kept worrying that I would be lonesome in my new apartment without her," says Ron, who separated from his wife a year ago. "Shelly kept offering to let me take one of her [stuffed] animal toys to keep me from being sad. But my teenage daughter just glared at me; she acted like the whole thing was a plot I'd hatched to ruin her life, I think." [33]

"Why couldn't you and dad have just waited?"

Teenagers whose parents are separating are usually more concerned with how the event will affect them. They might

			State-by-State Divorce Rates				
Rank	State	Number of Divorces	Rate per 1000	Rank	State	Number of Divorces	Rate per 1000
1	Massachusetts	14,530	2.4	26	Kansas	12,093	4.7
2	Connecticut	9,095	2.8		Utah	8,999	4.7
3	New Jersey	23,899	3.0	28	Delaware	3,385	4.8
4	Rhode Island	3,231	3.2	29	Montana	4,153	4.9
5	New York	59,195	3.3	30	Missouri	26,324	5.0
	Pennsylvania	40,040	3.3		West Virginia	9,179	5.0
7	Wisconsin	17,478	3.4	32	North Carolina	36,292	5.1
	North Dakota	2,201	3.4		Colorado	18,795	5.1
9	Maryland	17,439	3.5	34	Georgia	37,001	5.2
10	Minnesota	16,217	3.6	35	Oregon	16,307	5.3
	Louisiana	***	3.6	36	Texas	99,073	5.4
12	Illinois	43,398	3.7	37	Alaska	3,354	5.5
13	District of Columbia	2,244	3.9	38	Washington	29,976	5.6
	Iowa	10,930	3.9	39	Mississippi	15,212	5.7
15	Nebraska	6,547	4.0	40	Kentucky	22,211	5.8
	Vermont	2,316	4.0		Arizona	23,725	5.8
17	Michigan	38,727	4.1	42	Florida	82,963	5.9
18	South Dakota	3,022	4.2	43	New Mexico	9,882	6.0
	South Carolina	15,301	4.2	44	Idaho	7,075	6.2
	Hawaii	4,979	4.2		Alabama	26,116	6.2
21	California	***	4.3	46	Indiana	***	6.4
22	Maine	5,433	4.4	47	Wyoming	3,071	6.5
	New Hampshire	5,041	4.4	48	Tennessee	34,167	6.6
24	Ohio	49,968	4.5	49	Oklahoma	21,855	6.7
25	Virginia	30,016	4.6	50	Arkansas	17,458	7.1
				51	Nevada	13,061	9.0

All data are by state of occurrence of divorce and not by state of residence.

***Note: All statistics are for 1994 except: California (1987), Indiana (1987), and Louisiana (1983).

worry about the possibility that they will have less money to spend or will be without a car to drive. One woman recalls that her daughter seemed more worried about her friends finding out than anything else. "Kris was just mortified that her friends would know that her parents split up," says Barb. "She worried about whether she should tell her friends, or try to keep the whole thing a secret. I found it baffling that she wasn't more worried about anything more important than what a bunch of fifteen-year-olds would say."[34]

One counselor recalls a sophomore in high school who was angry that her parents were divorcing before she was done with high school. "She kept saying, 'I don't know why they couldn't have waited until I went to college—it wouldn't be as big a deal then!' It sounded completely self-centered, but I understood what she was saying.

"And it's so completely in character for an adolescent—the need for things to be on her own terms. She knew her parents didn't get along, and maybe even agreed that divorce was best. But she didn't want it interfering with what she viewed as a very important part of her life."[35]

Lawyers and decisions

At the same time teens and their younger siblings are worrying about the changes their parents' separation brings, the parents themselves are working out the details of the end to their marriage. Divorce involves problems that are not only emotional, but legal. Responsibilities that were shared by the couple need to be sorted out between two households, instead of one.

Each partner usually hires a lawyer to help with these arrangements. Often teens are confused by the idea of parents needing lawyers in dealing with one another; the presence of lawyers conjures up images of dramatic courtroom scenes and stern judges, and that is at odds with how parents make decisions at home.

Experts say, however, it is a wise idea for couples to use the services of lawyers because there are a number of issues in a divorce that can cause a great deal of controversy.

Deciding how property and finances should be divided or how responsibility for raising the children should be handled, for example, are such difficult questions that husbands and wives cannot work out without assistance. Explaining this to their teenage children can help them understand how crucial such assistance is.

After watching her lawyer, her husband's lawyer, and the judge in their first confrontation in court, one Michigan woman suddenly understood how critical lawyers are to the process of ending a marriage. "I realized that there was a language, a protocol, a ritual occurring that had little to do with our case but completely impacted on it. I then understood why you don't represent yourself in court. . . . Lawyers know the game that is being played and that's what you are paying for."[36]

Experts recommend that couples seeking a divorce consult with lawyers before making any decisions about finances, property, or child custody.

A process turned sour

Unfortunately, however, the process sometimes turns sour. A court case with lawyers is by nature adversarial; that is, lawyers try to get as much as possible for their client—whether it be child support payments, ownership of the family car, or custody of the children. Often when the parents are nursing anger and hurt feelings that led to their breakup in the first place, they continue to quarrel over these issues and urge their lawyers to "get all you can" from the other spouse. This attitude can escalate quickly, creating an unpleasant situation for both parents and their children.

Barbara, divorced three years ago, remembers well how the legal issues turned into a very expensive battleground between her husband and herself. "Tom and I weren't at each other's throats like some couples," she says. "We had agreed on the divorce because we just didn't love one another—not because either of us had cheated or anything. It seemed like the whole court thing was just a formality for us—we'd already decided to share custody of Matt, our son.

"But my attorney was overeager, I guess, and Tom's was no better. It seemed like they sort of took over, and before either of us knew what had happened, there were all sorts of petitions being filed, and Tom was angry because I was demanding more than I had agreed on. It's really amazing how it happened, escalating totally out of our control. I don't even like to think about how many thousands of dollars we spent."[37]

"He started saying stuff to me about my mom"

As emotionally draining as such battles are for parents, children feel even more of the stress. Although the parents may be separated during the legal battles, the hostility frequently carries over into their dealings with their children. Intentionally or not, one parent may display negative feelings regarding the estranged spouse to a youngster.

"My dad was real upset because he thought my mom was asking for way too much money in their divorce," says one fifteen-year-old. "He lived about a mile away from our house right after they got separated, and I'd go over there a couple afternoons a week after school. He's a writer and he works at home, so he's almost always there.

"Anyway, I thought things were good between my dad and me, but he got weird about things like money and some of the things he and my mom had bought over the years, like the big piano in our living room. He started saying stuff to me about my mom whenever I was over there, how she was trying to bleed him dry. He'd tell me how stupid she was about money, and how he used the piano more than she did, so he should get it. It got to where I just didn't go over to see him anymore. I hated listening to it."[38]

"The ugliest litigation"

The most unpleasant legal battles by far are about who will have custody, or responsibility, for the children after the divorce. Because custody battles by definition involve children directly, they are known to counselors and therapists as "the ugliest litigation." In the view of these health

Most counselors discourage couples from engaging in custody battles, as they are emotionally painful for all parties involved.

professionals, custody fights are not worth the damage they cause.

"For all you divorcing parents planning to get involved in custody battles," advises noted psychiatrist and children's advocate Melvin Goldzband, "the word is, *Don't*. Custody battles are strictly no-win situations. Regardless of who comes out on top in court, both parents and their children lose." [39]

Custody issues taken to court are ultimately decided by a judge, who, no matter how sincere and kind, is a stranger. He or she will take very little time to decide something that is of monumental importance to the family. Supposedly custody decisions are to reflect what is best for the child, but that is almost always a very difficult thing to ascertain—as evident from the changes in the way custody has been awarded over the years.

Father is best? Mother is best?

The idea of who should take over the responsibility of raising the children has gone through drastic changes in the United States. In the eighteenth and nineteenth centuries, children were considered the property of their fathers; therefore, when parents divorced, the father always got custody. It was believed that fathers were far better able to provide for the children financially—and that was the only consideration.

At the beginning of the twentieth century, there was a shift in the way homes (and families) were organized. With a more industrial society replacing the agrarian one, the nuclear family of mother, father, and children replaced the extended families that had been so common years before. It was more common for the father to leave the house to go to work, while the mother stayed home to keep the house and look after the children.

Each parent's role in child rearing became more narrowly defined; as a result, the courts began to favor the argument that mothers had an inborn ability to nurture children, especially in the child's early years. Judges began awarding custody of the children to mothers, in almost every instance. The father, according to clinical psychologist Edward Teyber, "was viewed as a breadwinner with no direct child-rearing role . . . [and] was issued alternate weekend visitation rights and required to pay alimony and child support to 'the family.'"[40]

Things changed again beginning around 1970. More women took jobs outside the home and more men took active parts in child rearing. Moreover, research by child psychologists showed how much children needed their fathers to be directly involved in their lives. As a result, the "only mother" and "only father" options in custody were replaced by a doctrine that custody should be determined by "the best interests of the child."

"Be forewarned"

In spite of attempts to keep the children's best interests in mind, it is not uncommon for a divorcing couple to disagree on how custody should be handled. Often initial disagreements about which parent has custody can be resolved between the parents themselves; in fact, more than 80 percent of custody cases are worked out in this manner.

"We each wanted sole custody of our sons," one mother recalls. "My husband and I were both very firm on that—and at first, we were willing to fight all the way on that point. But the judge in our divorce case absolutely insisted we work it out; she said she did not want it to go to court. So we did—we agreed on joint custody, where we alternate weeks with the boys. Neither of us was satisfied, but at least it was better than the other one getting sole custody, I guess."[41]

In those cases where parents can't agree on what's best for their children, the decision is made by the courts. Parents testify against one another, witnesses are called—all with the goal of making one parent look better than the other. Unfortunately, what usually happens, say divorce lawyers, is that parents try to make themselves look good by making their spouse appear unfit to raise a child.

Everyone—even the lawyers who gain financially from extended court battles—seems to agree that such custody

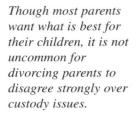

Though most parents want what is best for their children, it is not uncommon for divorcing parents to disagree strongly over custody issues.

battles are indeed "the ugliest litigation." Writes attorney Elliot Samuelson, "Be forewarned: Custody litigation is not for the fainthearted and should, wherever possible, be avoided. It is destructive to all persons who participate in the process. . . . It further exacerbates raw wounds of both father and mother."[42]

"I hate what you're doing to me"

Parents may get hurt, but teens who have lived through custody battles say that the worst thing about them is that they put kids in the middle of an ugly dispute between the two people they love the most.

"My mom and dad both wanted custody of us," says Tina, sixteen, whose parents divorced four years ago. "My sister and I were living with my mom—my dad had left. But he was determined that he'd get custody. I remember him talking to his lawyer on the phone about stuff, like how my mom was an unfit parent. He'd make lists, like of the little things she'd done wrong over the years." Tina tells how she got very angry one night when her father asked her about the time she'd broken her arm. "He was like, 'Wasn't that the time your mom let you Rollerblade without your [knee and elbow] pads?' He was trying to make it sound like it was her fault I broke my arm, and he was putting it down as another black mark against her, I guess. I just screamed at him—I think that was the first time I ever had the guts to do that. I told him, 'I hate what you're doing to me!' "[43]

A difficult determination

The ultimate goal of a custody decision is for the children to be safe and their lives to be disrupted as little as possible. Although this sounds good, how to achieve that goal is very difficult to determine, especially for a judge who has no prior association with the family.

To help judges make such decisions, some states hire family therapists to put together profiles by interviewing the children themselves, in addition to parents, teachers, grandparents, and friends. This is meant to give a better picture of the family and indicate what would be in that child's best interest.

Then the court therapists send their recommendations to the judges, who are often grateful for the input. "After we pull all this together, we have a pretty good picture of how the whole family is functioning, not just where the child is or what the divorce issues are," explains a child advocate in Tucson, Arizona. "We can't really put the family back together, but we can make a better judgement as to where the child is going to prosper better."[44]

Court therapists are sometimes employed to help determine a child's best interest in custody cases.

"I spent a lot of time just shrugging my shoulders"

Sometimes children are more directly involved in the custody decision. In cases where teenagers are involved, a judge may ask them what they prefer. Would they be happier living with their mother or their father? "The judge asked me that question," says Judd, now seventeen. "He asked me what it was like at home, was there a lot of hostility and stuff. He asked about if my mom was home at night, and about my dad's apartment—if I'd be comfortable there. But I don't think I helped the judge very much—I didn't really know what to say. I mean, you don't want to say anything that would make your parents feel bad. So I guess I spent a lot of time just shrugging my shoulders."[45]

Many child advocates say that asking teens about their preference puts them in an awkward position and gives them power they would probably rather not have. "No matter what," writes one expert, "they will prefer their first choice of having both parents together. Asking their choice of parent and living arrangements puts incredible pressure on [them], because they must hurt one parent terribly." [46]

"Something was decided, finally"

Instead, say counselors, it is far better for parents to settle custody without putting teens on the spot. Even if the solution is less than what either parent hoped, the most important thing is that teens and younger children understand that "home" has a different look than before, but it will be home nonetheless.

"By the time my husband and I, together with our lawyers and the judge, had sat for hours and hours over the course of three months battling it out, he and I realized we were killing ourselves," says one woman. "Neither of us got exactly what we wanted, but it was a workable compromise. It wasn't so much *what* we got, but that something was decided, finally. The best thing we could do for our daughters—as well as for ourselves—was to get it behind us and move on." [47]

3

Where Do
I Live Now?

ONCE THE DECISIONS are finally made—about
custody as well as property, child support payments, alimony, and other issues—the divorce proceedings are con-
cluded. However, even though the marriage is legally
over, the difficulties faced by teens whose parents have
just divorced are not over. In fact, the months and years
after the divorce, when teens and their families must get
used to different living arrangements, present a whole set
of difficult challenges.

What custody really means

Custody is usually thought of as a living arrangement,
but the term refers to much more. There is legal custody,
and there is physical custody. Legal custody refers to the
person or persons responsible for making important decisions about the upbringing of the children of the divorced
couple. Such decisions may include the types of medical
care, religious training, discipline, and education.

In sole legal custody, such decisions are made by the
parent with whom the children reside. In joint legal custody, both parents share in important decisions about
their children, even though the children may live with one
parent.

Physical custody refers to the actual living arrangement
of the family. Like legal custody, physical custody may be
granted to one parent or to both. Joint physical custody

means that children might split their time between two homes. Sole custody means that the children live with either their mother or their father, but have set times when they visit the noncustodial parent. In addition, the noncustodial parent is responsible for sharing the financial burden of raising the children. This is done through a monthly payment commonly called "child support," the amount of which is decided at the time of the divorce.

Sole custody

Despite the changes that have taken place in American family life since the early 1970s, when sole custody is granted in the United States, it is the divorced mother who most often gets custody. As of 1998, divorced fathers have sole custody in fewer than 15 percent of divorce cases. The reason for this is that mothers are still most often the primary caregivers, and when courts must choose one parent, they usually choose the one who spent the most time caring for the children before the divorce.

There are exceptions, of course. Some parents have physical or psychological problems that make sole custody impractical. Some are denied sole custody because of substance abuse issues. Some parents have jobs that prevent them from being able to care for their children as a sole custodian.

Fourteen-year-old Ryan's parents divorced when he was twelve. Since that time, he and his younger sister have lived with their father—an arrangement that Ryan says is working, for the most part. "It isn't so bad." Ryan shrugs. "We see my mom every other weekend, and two weeks in the summer. She travels a lot with her job, so in a way, I don't feel like I see her any less than before she and my dad split up. She calls us every night, even when she's in New York on business, and that's good. I mean, I wish they weren't divorced, but if they have to be, this way is OK."[48]

Sometimes for teens, the question of "Who?" is not as important as "Where?" Fifteen-year-old Tasha says that she didn't care that much which of her parents she lived with, as long as she didn't have to leave the neighborhood.

"All my friends are there," she says. "I told my mom and dad, 'I'll stay with whoever gets the house.' I wasn't kidding—my parents are both nice people, so I didn't want to choose. I figure I'll see a lot of whoever it is I don't live with, too, since my parents' houses are like six miles from one another. But I told them just leave me where I am, and let me be with my friends."[49]

Visitation

Even though the children live with one parent, however, experts stress that it is very important for them to have contact with their other (noncustodial) parent. At the time of the divorce, parents, and in some cases the judge, work out a schedule for children, regardless of their age, to see their other parent. For teens, many judges advise a schedule of every other weekend with the noncustodial parent—perhaps from after school on Friday to Sunday night. To this is added a few weeks during summer vacation.

Counselors emphasize that it is important for parents to be especially flexible with teens where visitation is concerned. They are busy people, with a variety of demands on their time. And while it is often easy to keep to a regimented schedule for younger children, teens often complain that such a schedule does not meet their needs. Such scheduling conflicts complicate an already emotionally complex relationship.

"I love going to my dad's—I do," insists one fourteen-year-old. "And most of the time, it's no problem to go to his place after school on Friday. I know my mom likes a little time to herself, and it's fine. But it seems like lately

Many children of divorced parents split their time between both parents.

the weekends I'm supposed to be at my dad's are when stuff is going on that I want to be home for—as in, home at my mom's. And then I feel guilty because Dad can tell I don't want to go to his house." [50]

"This little tiny window of opportunity to see Mom"

Sometimes teens feel somehow victimized by custody and visitation arrangements. Denny, sixteen, agrees. He and his younger brother live with their father. His mother, a lawyer, spends a great deal of time traveling between New York City and London; Denny's parents agreed before their divorce that the boys would feel more comfortable living with their father most of the time.

"I feel like we've got this little tiny window of opportunity to see Mom," he says. "It's like, 'That's all you get.' I hate that, because when it's our time to see her, we've got to go whether it's a good time for us or not. Why does everything have to depend on whether it's a good time for them, and not for us?

"I wish I could see her when I wanted to—it would be more often than seven days a month, that's for sure. It just wouldn't be all lined up on the calendar. I mean, how do you know when you need to see your mom or your dad? How can they know that in advance? I wish we all lived together, so I could see either of them whenever I wanted, but I know that's impossible." [51]

"It was like I was some family friend"

While the children of divorced parents may dislike the regimentation that scheduled visits impose, many noncustodial parents find the arrangements awkward as well. One of the most common complaints among such parents is that seeing their children only on preset dates is artificial, and that they feel as though they are the "second-best parent."

One divorced father describes how he felt like a stranger when he pulled up in front of his former residence to pick up his two children for a weekend visit. "I'd always con-

sidered myself a great father," he says. "But there I was, feeling really out of place when I knocked on the door. It was like I was some family friend or an uncle or something, rather than a dad. I hated the situation, and I could tell my kids did, too!"[52]

Psychologists say that such a reaction is perfectly normal, considering the change in roles that noncustodial parents undergo. "They go from being a parent on a daily basis to an ex-parent," says one counselor. "A lot of men, in particular, who only have visitation with their children feel as though they are divorced not only from their wives but from their children as well."[53]

It is not unusual for children to feel neglected or unloved when parents miss or cancel a scheduled visitation.

Broken plans, broken hearts

There are other problems with visitation that affect teens and younger children at least as much as the parents themselves. Parents who cancel or miss their scheduled times with their children risk giving the impression that they have stopped loving them or that they place little or no value on their feelings. Sometimes this is done intentionally, as when a parent seems to withdraw from the children out of anger at the other parent. For instance, if a noncustodial father feels that breaking his visitation commitment will inconvenience his ex-wife, he might invent excuses to do just that.

Sixteen-year-old Tom recalls how his own father canceled plans with him and his sister regularly. "It bothered me a lot," he says. "I didn't cry like my sister did, but she was only five or six when this happened all the time. My dad was supposed to pick us up after work on Thursdays—that's when my mom would be working—and we would go to his apartment and do stuff. A lot of times he called at the last minute and told my mom he had to change his plans, and so we just stayed home instead.

"It was like that for a long time. After a while, he didn't even call to say he wasn't coming to get us. My sister had these big fits where she'd just freak—crying and screaming and even hitting at my mom. I just acted sort of quiet. Inside, I felt really bad. And when my dad moved to Portland, over a thousand miles away, I wasn't surprised. My counselor said, 'Oh, this has nothing to do with you—it's your mom he's angry with,' but I didn't care. I was the one who felt bad, not my mom." [54]

"The trip home was always awful"

Sometimes, however, withdrawal by the noncustodial parent is not due to irresponsibility or forgetfulness. There are circumstances in which the process of visitation is so artificial, so uncomfortable, that many noncustodial parents simply back away. One father recalls how painful and how difficult it was for him making the 300-mile trip to see his three daughters after his divorce: "Every trip to see them was difficult because of the drive, anxiety about how the kids would be, and the difficulties with my ex-wife. The kids and I would go to a motel, get reacquainted, and in the two days I'd feel like a father again.

"The trip home was always awful, and I'd have to readjust to the loss of them again. I finally decided it would be easier for all to stop the trips. I always sent my support check and I never missed a birthday or Christmas. As I didn't know what to buy them, I'd just send checks."

But even though his "disappearance" from the lives of his children was not intended to hurt them, he says, he knows that it did indeed cause his children a great deal of unhappiness. "When the kids were grown," he continues, "each came to me separately and let me know how much they resented my disappearance from their lives. Each let me know that they would have preferred the pain of the visits to my having become just a 'check' in their lives." [55]

Counselors and youth advocates remind parents during the divorce process how important promises are, and how devastating it is to both young children and teens when they are broken. Even when the withdrawal is unintentional rather than aggressive, it can still cause emotional damage.

There are a number of other problems with the sole custody arrangement besides visitation schedules. From the custodial parent's point of view, it is a great deal more difficult to raise children and maintain a household alone than with a supportive spouse present. Many divorced single mothers find that raising children is far more stressful without a partner. It is very common to see such single parents suffer from what psychologists often term "role overload."

Role overload

Role overload simply means that one parent is doing the work of two parents—and is being stretched too far. The divorced mother who is working and raising children alone is particularly vulnerable to this problem, say experts. "They have to do it all," explains one psychologist, "go to work, clean the gutters and mow the yard, take care of the children every day, find time to take them to school or to the doctor, and do everything else." [56]

Despite the best intentions, without another parent around to lend emotional support, children—especially teens—can be too much of a challenge for the overworked parent. "Teenagers can be tough on parents even in the most stable two-parent families," explains one counselor. "They push limits, they test, they argue, they do what they're supposed to do developmentally at that age. And all that pushing and arguing and testing is very stressful to the parent when she has no one to back her up, no one to commiserate with when the teen starts yelling and slamming doors and being difficult. Parents desperately need that support from one another."[57]

Ironically, at the same time the single parent is adjusting to such a demanding role, teens and younger children have heightened needs for consistency and support, which they often don't receive. A single parent who is worrying about finances, balancing job and children, and emotionally drained from a divorce may find that the children receive less time than before the divorce. This lack of supervision can create additional problems. "Researchers have found that divorced mothers do not have as much time for their children," says psychologist Ed-

Saddled with greater financial burdens and more household responsibilities after a divorce, some parents find it difficult to give their children the attention they would like.

ward Teyber. "Divorced mothers also monitor their children less closely than mothers in two-parent homes. They know less about where their children are, who they are with, and what they are doing."[58]

Joint custody

The solution to the troubles that can arise in sole custody seems evident—give both parents strong roles in raising the children. This alternative to sole custody is joint custody—sometimes called "shared custody"—in which children alternate their time somewhat equally between parents. The idea behind this arrangement is that children have more regular and equal access to both parents.

Jake, sixteen, and his brother alternate months with their parents, who live twenty miles apart—although in the same school district. Although he balked at the arrangement at first, Jake says that he now enjoys the fact that he's got two separate homes. "I have friends that alternate weeks, but this month arrangement is better, I think," he says. "It gives me time to really feel comfortable, really settle in. My mom and my dad have both let me get my room in each place just how I like it."[59]

Another teen, fifteen-year-old Douglas, agrees. "Actually I kind of like the two homes," he admits. "When I seem to have worn out my welcome at one place, it's time to change and I start out fresh with the other parent."[60]

Equal access, unequal time

But while some joint custody situations involve alternating weeks or months between two homes, some do not. Advocates of joint custody emphasize that it is common for parents sharing custody of their children to have very different amounts of time with them. For example, a teen may spend far more time at his mother's home than at his father's. Such an arrangement differs from sole custody in that both parents are equally accessible to the children. This means that although the teen lives most of the time at his mother's, he is allowed—encouraged—to spend time at his father's house when he wants to. Both parents have a

Joint custody allows both parents to have strong roles in raising their children.

say in the kind of discipline used, his schooling, and other important aspects of his life.

"I don't think of myself as a single parent," says one divorced mother. "My ex and I are actively involved in Tim's school, in church activities, and we both help out on his baseball team with driving kids to games. Our marriage wasn't so hot, but somehow we've worked together for Tim's sake to make sure neither of us loses the closeness of our son."[61]

Seeing their parents put aside many of their differences to ensure the welfare of their children makes a big difference to many teens. Fifteen-year-old Toni observes: "They are really good about everything. I've got friends whose parents have split, and they say they feel like they're being fought over all the time. But my mom and dad are great. If my sister and I want to be at Dad's, we just clear it with Mom, and it's cool. It's never like, 'No, it's my weekend to have you,' or whatever."[62]

When it doesn't work

Judges often favor joint custody as a solution to custody disputes because it avoids appointing one parent as the "main" parent—while the other parent is left without a strong role in the upbringing of the children. These judges feel that joint custody is a compromise in which no one is left out. However, many psychologists worry that in finding an easy solution for custody disputes, judges may sometimes be doing more harm than good. Experts worry, for example, about parents who cannot get along without arguing or finding fault. In their view, such parents are unlikely to have the ability to orchestrate the hefty responsibility of raising children.

The results of inappropriately granted joint custody are evident from a 1990 study of high-conflict families done by the Center of Families in Transition in Corte Madera, California. When children of arguing, embittered parents were in joint custody situations, therapists and teachers found that these children tended to be more withdrawn, depressed, aggressive, or otherwise disturbed than were their counterparts in sole-custody situations.

Those who work with teens agree that joint custody, even if it seems like a good idea, just isn't in some cases. "I see joint custody get misused all the time," says one adolescent counselor. "I really believe that judges are often unable to make a decision about the proper call for custody—and so I think a lot of them say, 'Oh, I'll let both parents share custody.' But how can we expect two angry adults who couldn't agree on anything, who couldn't make a marriage work—how can we presume that they will suddenly become cordial co-workers in the most important job of all: raising children?"[63]

What's best?

Is there a "best" form of custody? Every family is different, so experts say there is no system that will work for everyone. Dean, sixteen, is a good example. His father has a history of violence and has physically and emotionally abused Dean and his mother. While many children would benefit greatly from spending time with both parents, the courts found that in Dean's case, it would be an endangerment.

"When I visited him, I saw him in the basement of the public library for an hour," says Dean. "That was four years ago, before he moved out of state—now I don't see him at all. But then, my dad's social worker or whatever sat in the same room with us. It was really weird. I didn't have that much to say to him, because I was pissed at him for hitting me all those times. But it still felt strange having a chaperone, like he was in prison or something."[64]

However, except in cases where a child might suffer abuse or harm by being with a parent, it is best for children to have as much contact and closeness as possible with both parents—no matter what type of physical custody arrangement is decided on.

"I know my parents can't stand each other," says one eighteen-year-old bluntly. "They divorced when I was twelve, and they haven't spoken many civil words to one another since then. But they kept us kids out of it, and they were always there for us, just not together. If I could have one piece of advice for parents who are divorcing, I'd say, 'If my parents could do that, you could, too. Just be there for your kids, and don't include them in your fights!'"[65]

Divorce mediator Genevieve Clapp agrees, "It is not so much the type of custody that is important. Rather, it is the absence of parental conflict and the quality of children's relationships with *both* parents that are important to children's well-being."[66]

4

Traps and Challenges

NO MATTER HOW agreeable parents and teens are to a custody situation, there are still a great many adjustments to be made on both sides when parents divorce. Problems are not always apparent early on; sometimes it is only after the family has lived in the new arrangement for a few months that trouble spots in the new way of life become evident.

The idea that divorce does not necessarily solve every problem and even creates new ones is disheartening to many teens. "I was sort of naive, I guess," says one sixteen-year-old. "I thought things would be better after they were apart; I assumed the fighting would be over, they wouldn't have anything to do with one another. But I was wrong!"[67]

Not much to look forward to

Much of the fighting centers around visitation. One parent brings the children back to the other late or changes plans, causing the other to be inconvenienced. And instead of being flexible, the other parent uses the occasion to stir up unpleasantness.

In her book *Helping Your Child Survive Divorce*, psychologist Mary Ann Shaw recounts the family situation of a thirteen-year-old boy named Austin. Glad to be away at camp and far from his divorced parents' constant battles, Austin is nervous when both of them come for the going home ceremonies. Afterward they fight—very publicly—about whose visitation time it is and who should drive him home, and Austin's nervousness quickly turns to humiliation as his peers witness the battle.

"What do kids like Austin have to look forward to?" asks Shaw. "High school graduation—it's a nightmare. A wedding? Holidays? Special occasions are just more opportunities for Mom and Dad to attack one another."[68]

In cases like this, some teens will eventually tend to avoid participating in anything—teams, church groups, theater productions—where their parents would both be present, just to avoid the unpleasantness it might cause. And though this avoidance might prevent some fighting, the teen will ultimately be the loser, missing out on a great deal of fun.

Fighting by proxy

Not all post divorce battles are public displays; in fact, some of the most unpleasant are waged in very private circumstances. Psychologists call this "fighting by proxy," for instead of having their arguments face-to-face, divorced parents often fight through their children.

Sometimes the fighting is initiated by the parent who feels wronged, who perhaps did not want the divorce in the first place. Having had no success in saving the marriage, that parent may try to enlist the children as allies against the other parent by saying negative things about the ex-spouse. "My mom was the worst offender," claims sixteen-year-old Anna. "Every chance she'd get, she'd remind us all of how my dad ended their marriage. Everything bad that happened after that was his fault, according to her. She'd say things like, 'You know, if your dad hadn't decided he wanted to be single again, we'd be able to afford to go up to the lake like we used to.' I don't really know if she knew how sickening that was—it was like she was trying to make us hate Dad."[69]

One thirteen-year-old explains that in his family, his father is guilty of fighting this way. Because his father feels that the child support and alimony payments are too high, he uses any excuse to belittle his ex-wife through his son. "He's always saying stuff about how much money she has—like if I go to his apartment with ripped jeans, he'll get mad. He says, 'I'm paying all that money each month, and this is what you wear?'"[70]

"[It] was making me a nervous wreck"

For such comments to be effective, of course, the parent who is being openly critical depends on the child to repeat them to the other parent. Thus, the children are quickly drawn into active roles in the ongoing fight. Sue, now twenty-one, remembers how she and her brother were willing pawns in the fighting-by-proxy game at first. "My dad would say things, and my brother and I would tell our mom," she recalls. "And then she'd get mad and say things, and we'd repeat them to Dad. They'd say, 'You tell your father such-and-such,' or, 'Ask your mother just why she does whatever.' It was always a criticism.

"Things changed for me when I talked to a counselor at my high school—because the whole situation was making me a nervous wreck. My counselor told me to explain to my parents I wasn't going to relay any more 'messages.' So I did. I told them how it made me feel, and how if they wanted to say things, they should pick up the

Children can sometimes get caught in the middle of parental disputes, leading them to struggle with loyalty issues.

Facts About Divorce

United States	Canada

Median age at divorce:
   males 35.6
   females 33.2
	Median age at divorce:
	   males 38
	   females 36

Median duration of marriage:
   7.2 years
	Median duration of marriage:
	   10 years

Estimated number of children involved in divorce: 1,075,000	Estimated number of dependant children involved in divorce: 36,252
Rate per 1,000 population of children under 18 involved in divorce: 16.8	

Source: National Center for Health Statistics and Canada Statistics.

phone (when I wasn't around, preferably) and say them to the other's face."[71]

Even though directness like this might not change their parents' behaviors, it is important for teens to at least tell them how they feel, say experts. Allowing such sniping will tend to make visitations unpleasant and stressful. Parents need to work hard at being civil about the other parent in the presence of teens and younger children—even if positive comments are somewhat forced. As one divorce expert advises parents, "It doesn't matter how you feel about the other parent; it only matters how you act."[72]

Bribery

Another way in which parents can "fight" without even speaking a word to one another is by competing for the affection of their teens and younger children. Parents who do this are not necessarily thinking of what is best for their children; rather, they are using their children as ammunition to hurt the other parent. Such competition is far more common than one might believe—and there are several ways parents go about it.

Sometimes a parent will spend money on lavish gifts—things the teen may have mentioned wanting but couldn't afford. Cars, clothes, sporting equipment—high-ticket items that were out of the question before—now are offered as presents. For some teens, the gifts are exciting; for others, the idea of such expensive presents is confusing. "My parents were into buying us," says one boy. "I used to see it all the time with other kids at my school, and it was sort of pathetic and obvious, you know? Like the mother would give her kid something really expensive, and then the dad would go out and try to top that—like get a car or something.

"Anyway, my parents did the same thing. It was sort of confusing, too. My parents used to be really big on not watching much television; they'd rather have us read books. But all of a sudden, my sister gets a color TV for

Divorced parents may buy their children expensive gifts out of guilt or as a way of competing with their ex-spouse for their child's affection.

her room! It would be like, OK—which is it? Do you really want us cutting down on TV or not? It was just about competition between Mom and Dad."[73]

"It's not always presents"

As with other forms of fighting by proxy, the children find themselves directly involved in the fight. After a summer vacation with her mother, Tina came home sporting a nose stud. Her father, who has custody of Tina and her brother, was livid. "I think that's the maddest I've ever seen him," Tina says. "And I know that I'm part to blame—well, maybe more than part. I knew my dad would never let me get one, and my mom was willing. That's it. She asked me if Dad would have a fit, and I sort of avoided answering. But she was kind of encouraging it, you know? She and my dad don't get along at all, and I think she figured she could get on my good side letting me do stuff I couldn't do otherwise."

Tina notes, too, that teens are not always equipped to avoid the conflict by refusing to get involved. "Some of the kids at my school get a lot of bribes from their parents when they get divorced, and they usually don't complain. I mean, would you? In a way, I think it brings out the worst in us, because we sort of know how to play it, you know? Like I know if I complain about my dad being really strict or not letting me wear a certain thing, or whatever, my mom is quick to get me something or give me special privileges. It's not always presents—sometimes the best bribes are like no curfews or things like that."[74]

Being "overburdened"

Not all excessive gift-giving is a means to hurt the other parent. Some divorced parents are struggling with guilt; they may feel bad for putting their children through such troubling times. Compensating by extending curfews or giving expensive presents may temporarily ease those guilty feelings somewhat.

Sometimes bribery is a sign that divorced parents are finding it difficult to cope with being alone or with the feeling as though they have been rejected. Occasionally such feelings make these parents needy—and they can turn to their children in inappropriate ways. Psychologists call teens in this situation "overburdened," for they are made to take on a bigger role in the family than they should.

There are several ways that divorced parents can overburden their teenage children. For example, a parent, needing emotional support, might pressure the teen to take her side in the ongoing disagreements between her and her ex-husband. One girl recalls how her mother would be angry with her when she returned from weekend visits with her father, for her mother thought she had "gone over to her dad's side." "My mom isn't like that anymore, but she used to be," she says. "I'd come home on Sunday night, and my mom would hardly speak to me. The first time it happened, I got scared—I thought, 'Did my teacher call or something?' I couldn't figure out what I had done. But then I figured out that she was mad because I'd been gone. She acted like I chose Dad over her." [75]

Teens as confidants

Another way divorced parents can overburden their teenagers is to treat them as peers—a phenomenon that psychologists report is becoming more and more common. A parent who is used to having a spouse to talk with often feels extremely lonely after a divorce and might look for a sympathetic ear in a teenage child. But while being treated as an adult may be somewhat flattering, teens are not emotionally equipped for serving as confidants of adults.

Lori, thirteen, had always had a close relationship with her mother, but found that relationship uncomfortably close after her parents' divorce. "My mom expected me to be around all the time," she complains. "Every time I'd leave the house, she acted really strange, like she thought we were going to spend the day together. Sometimes we did, and it was OK. But I didn't want to stop seeing my own friends. It's like my mom decided I was going to be her new best friend, and I didn't want that—and it sort of made me feel guilty, because she's my mom, you know?" [76]

Parents who are used to having a spouse as a confidant may turn to their teenagers as a source of support after a divorce.

"We sort of switched places"

Sometimes it's the teen's time the needy parent wants; other times it's the emotional support that used to be provided by the spouse. One boy, who was twelve when his parents divorced, has lived with his mother for the past five years, seeing his father only once or twice a month. However, it was his mother who seemed to need him most, he says. "I knew she was hurting after the divorce, because Dad had had an affair with a nurse at work. That's why they got divorced. And I guess I felt like if Dad wasn't around, I had to keep her from feeling bad. She'd get into these moods where she'd just want to sleep or she'd be really emotional, crying all the time.

"So I stayed home a lot and took care of her. Now I know that it wasn't good for me, because what happened was we sort of switched places. I made food she liked; I made sure she got up for work on time. I was the parent, and she was the kid."[77]

Other times a teen is enlisted as a surrogate mother or father for a younger brother or sister, or as an adviser on a parent's other personal problems. Without the built-in support that a spouse provides, a single parent may lack the confidence to make strong decisions about various aspects of day-to-day life. As a result, the parent may ask the advice of a teenage child.

"I hear these parents quite frequently," says one therapist. "They look at their teenage sons and daughters and say, 'Should we let Mary Ann go to that party?' or, 'What should we do about your little brother's cheating on his spelling test?' Or they may ask the teen's opinion about a problem with their boss at work, or some other matter.

"And it's wrong. Parents need to understand that leaning on an older child in this way may be a comfort for them, but it's not good for the teenager. Teens are not husband or wife substitutes. They are kids, who need the freedom to be kids. By abandoning the power of adulthood to fifteen-year-olds, a parent runs a great risk of doing serious emotional harm to that teenager."[78]

The importance of generational boundaries

Psychologists and therapists often remind divorced parents to maintain what they call "generational boundaries" between themselves and their older children. It's fine, they say, to share some of their problems or concerns with their teenage children, but it is not right to abandon their parental role. "Many children have already lost one parental figure through divorce," explains one expert. "They cannot afford to lose the other as well. Children and adolescents need their single parents to be in charge and to provide them with discipline, limits, and guidelines."[79]

If such discipline isn't provided, teens whose roles in the family have been blurred may have real problems later on. Accustomed to making or sharing in decisions, they may rebel against authority when it is applied—in school or at a job, for instance. And because they have learned to fill roles ordinarily reserved for adults, they may feel that they are too grown up for the friends and activities that once suited them.

"I made that mistake with my son," admits one mother. "I expected him to fill too big a role at home, and since he never complained, I figured it was all right. He was even making budget decisions for us—I'm embarrassed to say. At fourteen!

"But eventually, I started hearing about his trouble at school, about fighting and even drinking—things he'd never done before. Kevin wasn't ready to be an adult, and the pressure of me treating him like one stressed him out. Fortunately, counseling helped us both."[80]

Staying afloat

But even when roles are understood and discipline established, there are some consequences of divorce that are for many families almost inevitable. Financial strain is one of those since parents now must support and maintain two separate households instead of one. That means that money becomes a sensitive issue, even in families where it never was before.

Many newly divorced custodial parents are stunned to realize how a divorce can lower their standard of living. In fact, many experts on the divorce process call the financial impact on families divorce's "best-kept secret."

Numerous studies have shown that the hardest hit of all are mothers and children; they are three times as likely to live in poverty as fathers. In 1990 Dr. Judith Wallerstein conducted a study that found that almost 29 percent of women with children under eighteen were living in poverty. Another study in 1991 found that the first year after a divorce, mothers and children experienced on average a 73 percent drop in their standard of living, whereas divorced men's standard of living rose by 42 percent.

Lacking child support

One of the most important reasons for this drastic disparity in divorce's consequences is the lack of regular child support payments made by fathers to custodial mothers.

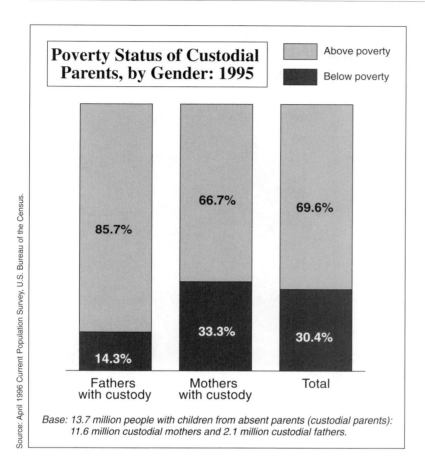

Source: April 1996 Current Population Survey, U.S. Bureau of the Census.

Poverty Status of Custodial Parents, by Gender: 1995

Above poverty
Below poverty

85.7%
66.7%
69.6%

14.3%
33.3%
30.4%

Fathers with custody
Mothers with custody
Total

Base: 13.7 million people with children from absent parents (custodial parents): 11.6 million custodial mothers and 2.1 million custodial fathers.

According to statistics compiled by the U.S. Census Bureau, more than $50 million in child support payments was unpaid in 1997. A fourth of the mothers and children that are supposed to receive regular support checks are not receiving any. Only half the fathers who are supposed to pay child support actually pay the full amount.

The reasons for the failure of fathers to pay child support are numerous. Often, fathers who are guilty of nonpayment feel resentment and think that they should not have to pay for children who no longer live with them. Anger with their former spouse colors their relationship with their children, and they come to believe that they should no longer be forced to send money to support them. Such fathers are often termed "deadbeat dads," although

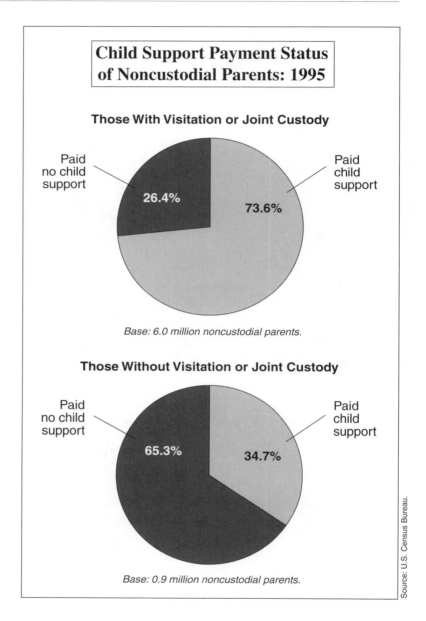

Child Support Payment Status of Noncustodial Parents: 1995

Those With Visitation or Joint Custody

Paid no child support

26.4%

Paid child support

73.6%

Base: 6.0 million noncustodial parents.

Those Without Visitation or Joint Custody

Paid no child support

65.3%

Paid child support

34.7%

Base: 0.9 million noncustodial parents.

Source: U.S. Census Bureau.

some contend that their failure to pay is a form of protest over their lack of access to their children. Of course, the ones caught in the middle when ex-spouses fight in this fashion are the children.

"See, they call us 'deadbeat dads,'" says one man who stopped making payments two years ago, "but that's really only one take on it. I admit I could be paying child support, but I don't now. I mean, she [my ex-wife] wanted the kids so bad she couldn't figure out a way to let me see them more than a couple times a month. And then if she was mad at me about something, she'd invent an excuse for me not to see them at all. Well, that wasn't any good for me. So she wants the kids, she's got 'em. And that's that, as far as I'm concerned. All I am is a damned bank, I guess, and that was unacceptable."[81]

A different way of life

The partial or nonpayment of child support, while a critical problem, is not the only reason for the financial difficulties experienced by divorced mothers and children. Many experts note that the amount needed by any parent increases as the children get older, but that this escalating need isn't taken into account when courts decide the amount of child support at the time of the divorce.

One mother complains that the amount she receives from her ex-husband has remained unchanged for four years—even though her children are teenagers now. "It's a lot different supporting three teenagers," she says. "When kids are little, it's so much easier to cut corners. But the amount I get from my ex doesn't make much of a dent in my expenses for my kids now. How do you factor in jeans, shoes—even a prom dress? All the extras add up."[82]

"It's just too much for me"

The answer, for many divorced mothers, is to "downsize"—everything from the car they drive to the home they live in with their children. For instance, while Terry's divorce settlement granted her the family home for herself and her children, she cannot maintain it on the money she makes—even though she receives regular child support checks. This financial situation can cause upheaval in the lives of the children—a fact that many parents recognize all too well.

"It's just too much for me," Terry says sadly. "Things break, things leak. I tried to do a lot of the patching and fixing up myself, but there's a limit to my time and my expertise. My kids and I found an apartment closer to the city, and that's where we live now. We don't have a yard, and it's hard to get used to neighbors on the other side of the wall! But at least we're in the same school district, so my thirteen-year-old won't have to struggle with a whole new school."[83]

Terry isn't alone; about 15 percent of divorced mothers find that they must move to less expensive housing after their divorce. For the children, such a move may mean a different neighborhood farther from their friends. And because single mothers are looking for less expensive housing, teens may find that this new neighborhood is less stable than the former one and that crime is more prevalent.

"My kids were good sports about the move at first," says Barb, a divorced mother of two. "And the neighborhood wasn't as nice as our old one, but it seemed quiet. But that was February! When it got to be spring and the weather was nicer, the neighborhood was not so nice. Lots of teenagers, lots of loud radios, lots of hanging around in the street outside our building. I know my girls were more than a little intimidated, and I felt very, very bad for them."[84]

New jobs, new responsibilities

There is another part of the financial picture for single mothers that frequently affects their teenage children. A large percentage of divorced mothers realize that they must earn more money to keep their household going. Many who did not work outside the home before the divorce get an outside job; those who worked part-time before quite often need to increase their hours to full-time.

The economics of working single mothers goes in two directions, say experts. For some who had careers before having families, the transition is not terribly difficult. However, those who have never worked outside the home find that their lack of education or experience severely limits their job opportunities. These women often must work for low wages and few benefits.

After a divorce, children might be asked to take on additional household responsibilities.

Because these working mothers need help balancing housework, childcare, and their outside jobs, teens may be asked to help out more at home than they did before the divorce. Starting dinner or taking care of younger siblings are frequent tasks that fall to teens—and some find it a problem.

"My mom works four nights a week as a waitress," says Ryan, fourteen. "She's tired when she gets home—usually after my little sister is in bed. I know the money helps, and she has to work. I was mad when she told me I had to come home from school Tuesdays, Thursdays, and Fridays to take care of Ellen. That meant I couldn't hang out with my friends. And in the winter, I couldn't try out for the middle school basketball team, because that's when the practices are." [85]

But other teens find that although the extra responsibilities are sometimes inconvenient, they feel good about helping. Sarah knows that her mother couldn't work and be home for her two youngest children after school, so Sarah took over this task. "I missed some things at school for a while," she admits. "But I really connected with my little brothers. We did things after school together, and most of the time it was OK to bring a friend home with me. I feel like I've been able to handle responsibility a lot better than some of my other friends." [86]

5

Trying to
Move Ahead

THERE IS NO question that divorce causes pain and anguish to the teenage children in the family. While divorced parents usually recover and move on with their lives within a year or two—often dating and marrying again—teens find it much more difficult to move on. Many experience effects that are long term—lasting well into adulthood.

Until quite recently, the consensus among counselors and other youth workers was that the harmful effects of divorce were overrated. Many experts insisted that a situation in which the parents were angry or unhappy all the time was far more harmful to teens and younger children than divorce would be. As long as parents presented the fact that they were splitting up in a reasonable, positive way, the thinking went, the children could accept the situation.

Many professionals stressed that young people's resiliency made them much tougher, much more flexible than most adults give them credit for. Rather than being monumental in its negative effects on teens and younger children, said University of Pennsylvania professor Frank Furstenburg Jr., "the overall effect of divorce is modest to moderate."[87]

Others are less certain that divorce is not traumatic. Joyce Borenstein, a Montreal filmmaker, was toying with the idea of doing a documentary on teens and divorce in 1993. Not sure if there was enough "substance" for the

While some teens adjust after their parents divorce, others experience long-term effects.

project to continue, she interviewed eighty young people whose parents had divorced. Borenstein was astonished to discover that the emotions the youngsters displayed were far more like grief than anything else. "I was witness to so much sadness and pain," she says. "I knew the film had to be done." [88]

A great deal of more recent research seems to point in another, more serious direction. Children of divorce may not be as resilient and flexible as once thought. And even though they do adjust to the weighty changes in their lives, they pay a sometimes frightening price.

Some of the most sobering research has been done by social scientist Judith Wallerstein. In the 1970s, Wallerstein began a study of 131 young people whose parents were divorcing. She noted the difficulties they were experiencing, such as depression and hostility. Wallerstein tracked those same young people eighteen months later, when she reported that "we didn't see a single child who was well-adjusted. And we didn't see a single child to whom divorce was not the central event of their lives."[89] Even more troubling, Wallerstein's further studies—five, ten, and fifteen years after their parents' divorces—found that many of the subjects remained troubled.

John Guidubaldi, past president of the National Association of School Psychologists, notes that while most children whose parents divorce adjust to the changes, that isn't what the real issue is. "For years experts said, 'Once the initial trauma wears off, kids make adjustments.' But so do people in prisons and mental institutions. The pertinent question is: Are those adjustments healthy? And the weight of the evidence has become overwhelming on the side that they aren't."[90] Even when the adjustment is a healthy one, pitfalls remain.

Loyalty issues

Statistics show that four out of five divorced people will marry for a second time. Such figures indicate that the main participants in divorce are ready to move on to a new chapter of their lives and find happiness. However, while teens may have made progress in dealing with the anger and hurt caused by their parents' split, a new person arriving on the scene can cause intense new problems. Most teens have been struggling with loyalty issues since before the divorce—uncertain as to which parent needed their support. A new love interest for one of their parents can make the question of loyalty even more muddled. What about the other parent: Will he or she be lonely or distraught?

"I was so angry the first time my dad went out on a date," admits one girl, fifteen. "I spent the whole time he was out—it was a picnic on a Saturday afternoon, I remember—up in my room, worrying. What was Mom going to say? Will she cry; will she be upset? I hated my dad for going out."[91]

Counselors know that during and after the divorce process, children of all ages harbor a hope that their parents will reconcile. Even teens, who are usually more aware of the reasons for the split, may harbor such hopes, although they may know intellectually that there is no chance of their parents getting back together. When a parent starts dating, that puts an end to the hope—however irrational—and that can be painful.

On and on

Such conflicts can often exist long after a parent remarries, creating loyalty issues well into a child's adult years. Brian, twenty, still feels anxiety during holidays because he doesn't want to have to choose between his father and stepmother and his mother. "My dad's remarried, and I'm welcome there," he says. "And that would be easiest, because that's close to where I live. But my mom has never gotten over my dad, and she's really needy. I always feel as though I need to be with her. And that pretty much ruins any excitement or anticipation about Christmas. I don't think I've looked forward to one since the divorce!"[92]

Others agree, citing nervousness about any family event, such as a baptism, wedding, or holiday, as an occasion for nervousness. "I'm so tired of worrying about my parents' feelings," admits one woman whose parents divorced thirty years ago. "I am an adult, with a career and family that are everything to me. Yet when I'm faced with the idea of planning my daughter's first communion party, with all of those bitter people in one house, I become a seven-year-old again."[93]

The "Sleeper Effect"

Researchers have also found that teens of divorced parents may experience a delayed reaction to the breakup. Teenage girls sometimes exhibit what psychologist Judith

Children of divorced parents sometimes seek out relationships to fulfill their need for approval and closeness.

Wallerstein calls the "Sleeper Effect." That means that although some girls seem to have adjusted quite well to their parents' divorce, a lot of turmoil and anger is merely buried—or sleeping—inside, ready to emerge years later. When girls get into their late teens and early twenties, they sometimes become convinced that no one really loves them or cares about them. They feel the need for approval and closeness, however, so they often seek those things through casual sexual encounters.

"After dealing with my parents' divorce," explains a twenty-one-year-old from Los Angeles, "I didn't feel like getting seriously involved with guys. So I hooked up with a *lot* of guys, thinking that would keep me from being hurt and vulnerable."[94]

Counselors warn that sexual relationships of this nature are a sign that the teen is hurting; they are also dangerous, both physically and emotionally. "This is not a good time to have many sexual partners anyway," explains one youth worker. "Young people need to worry about AIDS and other diseases. Add to that the eventual feelings of shame and low self-worth the teen will experience, and it's a bad, bad situation."[95]

Relationship anxiety

Another symptom of the Sleeper Effect is intense apprehension about relationships that could turn serious. Many avoid commitments, believing that they are unlovable or unlucky. Many teens admit that after seeing their parents get divorced, they had doubts about their own abilities to evaluate relationships and boys.

"My first boyfriend, Mark, and I spent every free moment together," recalls one young woman. "The only problem was that no matter how many times he said he loved me, I never believed him. And every time we disagreed about something, I was sure he was going to dump me. At first I thought that I was just majorly insecure. But when I felt equally apprehensive about my next boyfriend, I started to worry that something was really wrong with me."[96]

It's different with boys

Although boys do not experience the Sleeper Effect, they often have long-term problems of a different nature. Since by far the majority of children live with their mother after a divorce, boys often are faced with having to grow up without a male role model. Without a father around to watch—whether it's working, doing things around the house, relating to friends and family members—boys are often muddled in their idea of how a man acts.

"Boys don't just grow up with a solid sense of their own masculinity," explains University of Michigan psychologist Neil Kalter. "They have to find someone to emulate. But even fathers who are involved with their sons after the divorce might be seeing them only every other week. That's not enough contact."[97]

And without such contact, boys may grow up to be young men with little or no confidence in committing to either jobs or relationships. In fact, Wallerstein's ten-year interviews revealed that approximately 50 percent of the young men or teen boys considered themselves unhappy and unsuccessful in establishing a romantic bond.

"It's not a given"

It would be wrong, however, to conclude that all teens whose parents divorce will lead unhappy lives. There are many teens who weather the changes very well. Psychologists believe there are a number of reasons why some come out of a divorce unscathed, while others have problems.

One of the keys to helping youngsters deal with divorce, say experts, is for the parents to help the teen maintain ties with grandparents and other adult relatives and friends after the divorce. Too often such relationships fall by the wayside—either because of tension in the family or because relocation after the divorce makes such visits impractical. The diminished contact with grandparents and other relatives is often very difficult for children.

Tom, whose parents divorced eighteen months ago, admits that he misses seeing his grandparents after the divorce. "They're my dad's parents," he explains. "And we live with my mom. She doesn't hate them or anything, but she's really mad at my dad—so she's not real happy about me going to see them.

"They have a cabin up north where Grandpa always took me fishing and snowshoeing. It seems like a big part of my life is gone, without having trips to the cabin to look forward to."[98]

Grandparents caught in the crossfire of divorce often feel the same sense of loss about their grandchildren.

"Nothing has brought me more pain in the last five years than the loss of my grandchildren," says one woman sadly. "I've been a part of every birthday, every holiday, every school game and concert. And now, because my daughter-in-law has custody and has moved to Chicago, we hardly see them. I find myself wondering, 'Do those kids miss me as much as I miss them?'"[99]

More than ever, teens and younger children whose parents are divorcing need the continuity and support of other loving adults—and grandparents and other relatives certainly fill that need. Unfortunately, many teens don't get that support. In Wallerstein's study, for example, fewer than 10 percent of the children had any adult—even a relative—to speak with them sympathetically as the divorce unfolded.

Children benefit from the support of other adults such as grandparents after their parents divorce.

Rules for parents

There is a second important factor that seems to distinguish teens who are damaged by divorce from those who

are not: the willingness and ability of their parents to place their children's well-being above their own disagreements.

"I know my parents don't love each other anymore," says one eighteen-year-old, philosophically. "And although I used to have these elaborate fantasies that they'd get back together like in the movie *The Parent Trap*, I'm over that. But they're better than a lot of divorced parents I know. They love me, and they've really worked on putting their relationship with me and my brother on a whole different level than their relationship with each other. That's really cool—they aren't threatened at all—*at all*—that I love them both." [100]

Parents need to learn what these parents learned—that although they are no longer married to one another, they are always going to be linked by their relationship to their children. "Most divorced parents take a very limited view of the future," says one family therapist. "They ask, 'How do we get through the divorce?' as if it were a single event. But it's something they will have to live with for the rest of their lives."

When counseling divorcing parents, therapists ask them to look to the future. A counselor explains: "I say, 'What will you do when you're grandparents, and there's a birth? How about your daughter's high school graduation two years from now?'" [101] Once parents understand how those occasions can be ruined by squabbles and arguments, they begin to understand that for the children, divorce is really never over.

Speak up

Those who work with people going through a divorce urge parents not to put children in the middle, not to use them as ammunition in spousal arguments, and so on. But because divorcing parents are frequently angry and bitter, they often do those things anyway—sometimes without even realizing it. For this reason, counselors and therapists also urge teens to speak up when they feel that parents are putting them in awkward or uncomfortable situations.

"Parents need to hear when they are acting more juvenile than their children," says one counselor. "A teen who

Talking about the feelings that accompany a divorce can help make the experience less painful for teens.

can respectfully, but firmly, look his father or mother in the eye and say, 'Hey, stop it, please—you're making me feel bad here,' will get more results than one parent saying it to the other. The parent will usually listen, and at least try to make things better." [102]

Things that work

In addition to speaking up to parents, there are other ways that teens can help themselves make the divorce process less traumatic. One is to simply talk about it—a therapy in itself. By verbalizing some of the feelings they have to friends, a teacher, or a counselor, teens can unload a lot of the hurt and anger that make them uncomfortable. Teens need to let go of the idea that the divorce makes them different or that it is something to be kept under wraps.

Surprisingly, talking to strangers about the anger and guilt one is feeling is often easier than talking to friends. There are support groups for teens and younger children whose parents are divorced. These are sometimes a more comfortable setting in which teens can voice the anxieties or emotions they are experiencing, since the members of the group are not necessarily people from school or the neighborhood.

The courts that handle divorce cases are also trying to help youngsters deal with divorces. For example, some cities and counties require divorcing parents and their children to attend a "course" in divorce. One such course that has helped tens of thousands of teens and younger children is called Sandcastles, the creation of Miami Beach therapist Gary Neuman.

At Sandcastles, counselors encourage young people to participate in interactive therapy—role-playing, drawing family pictures, and writing letters to their parents. Such activities help teens and younger children identify the fears they have—and allow them to vent some of the anger they feel. One boy who participated in the course learned something that made him feel relieved. "I thought I was part of the problem," he says. "Now I know I'm not." [103]

"In the very air we breathe"

Even if a teen is fortunate to have parents who are happily married, divorce is still a part of his or her world. Most young people have good friends whose parents are divorced—it is simply a fact of life. As one researcher comments, "Divorce is in the very air we breathe." [104]

The more teens understand about the effects of divorce on their parents and people their own age, the more supportive they can be when a friend or classmate is going through family turmoil. How teens react to such pain, how strong and helpful they can be when faced with it in others, can sometimes make all the difference to the one who is dealing with the uncertain future resulting from divorce.

Notes

Introduction

1. Interview by author, Hudson, Wisconsin, June 1999.
2. Barbara Dafoe Whitehead, *The Divorce Culture*. New York: Alfred A. Knopf, 1997, p. 82.
3. Interview by author, Minneapolis, Minnesota, June 1999.
4. Whitehead, *The Divorce Culture*, p. 82.
5. Interview by author, Minneapolis, Minnesota, June 1999.

Chapter 1: Cracks in the Foundation

6. Interview by author, Bloomington, Minnesota, June 1999.
7. Interview by author, Minneapolis, Minnesota, June 1999.
8. Interview by author, St. Paul, Minnesota, April 1996.
9. Interview by author, White Bear Lake, Minnesota, June 1999.
10. Interview by author, Hopkins, Minnesota, July 1999.
11. Interview by author, Minneapolis, Minnesota, June 1999.
12. M. Gary Neuman, *Helping Your Kids Cope with Divorce the Sandcastles Way*. New York: Times Books, 1998, p. 160.
13. Interview by author, Edina, Minnesota, June 1999.
14. Telephone interview by author, July 1999.
15. Interview by author, Bloomington, Minnesota, June 1999.
16. Interview by author, Edina, Minnesota, September 1999.
17. Interview by author, Edina, Minnesota, June 1999.

18. Interview by author, Edina, Minnesota, June 1999.

19. Telephone interview by author, July 1999.

20. Interview by author, Minneapolis, Minnesota, February 1996.

21. Telephone interview by author, July 1999.

22. Quoted in Marlien Rentmeester, "Splintered Families," *Seventeen*, December 1997, p. 163.

23. Quoted in Rentmeester, "Splintered Families," p. 163.

24. Telephone interview by author, July 1999.

Chapter 2: The Mechanics of Divorce

25. Interview by author, St. Paul, Minnesota, July 1999.

26. Interview by author, Minneapolis, Minnesota, June 1999.

27. Interview by author, St. Paul, Minnesota, July 1999.

28. Interview by author, Minneapolis, Minnesota, July 1999.

29. Telephone interview by author, June 1999.

30. Mary Ann Shaw, *Helping Your Child Survive Divorce*. Secaucus, NJ: Birch Lane Press, 1997, p. 26.

31. Interview by author, St. Paul, Minnesota, June 1999.

32. Anthony E. Wolf, *"Why Did You Have to Get a Divorce? And When Can I Get a Hamster?"* New York: Noonday Press, 1998, p. 35.

33. Interview by author, St. Paul, Minnesota, June 1999.

34. Interview by author, Bloomington, Minnesota, July 1999.

35. Telephone interview by author, July 1999.

36. Quoted in Vicki Lansky, *Vicki Lansky's Divorce Book for Parents: Helping Your Children Cope with Divorce and Its Aftermath*. New York: New American Library, 1989, p. 122.

37. Interview by author, Minneapolis, Minnesota, July 1999.

38. Interview by author, Minneapolis, Minnesota, June 1999.

39. Melvin Goldzband, *Quality Time: Easing the Children Through Divorce*. New York: McGraw-Hill, 1985, p. 21.

40. Edward Teyber, *Helping Children Cope with Divorce.* New York: Lexington Books, 1992, p. 119.

41. Interview by author, St. Paul, Minnesota, July 1999.

42. Quoted in Genevieve Clapp, *Divorce and New Beginnings: An Authoritative Guide to Recovery and Growth, Solo Parenting, and Stepfamilies.* New York: John Wiley and Sons, 1992, p. 166.

43. Interview by author, St. Paul, Minnesota, July 1999.

44. Quoted in Linda Bird Francke, *Growing Up Divorced.* New York: Linden Press, 1983, p. 255.

45. Telephone interview by author, July 1999.

46. Lansky, *Divorce Book for Parents*, p. 127.

47. Interview by author, St. Paul, Minnesota, July 1999.

Chapter 3: Where Do I Live Now?

48. Interview by author, Bloomington, Minnesota, July 1999.

49. Telephone interview by author, June 1999.

50. Interview by author, Minneapolis, Minnesota, June 1999.

51. Telephone interview by author, July 1999.

52. Interview by author, Bloomington, Minnesota, June 1999.

53. Interview by author, Edina, Minnesota, July 1999.

54. Interview by author, Minneapolis, Minnesota, June 1999.

55. Quoted in Lansky, *Divorce Book for Parents*, p. 149.

56. Teyber, *Helping Children Cope with Divorce*, p. 96.

57. Telephone interview by author, July 1999.

58. Teyber, *Helping Children Cope with Divorce*, p. 97.

59. Interview by author, St. Paul, Minnesota, July 1999.

60. Quoted in Lansky, *Divorce Book for Parents*, p. 169.

61. Interview by author, St. Paul, Minnesota, July 1999.

62. Telephone interview by author, June 1999.

63. Telephone interview by author, July 1999.

64. Telephone interview by author, September 1999.

65. Interview by author, Minneapolis, Minnesota, June 1999.

66. Clapp, *Divorce and New Beginnings*, p. 136.

Chapter 4: Traps and Challenges

67. Interview by author, St. Paul, Minnesota, July 1999.

68. Shaw, *Helping Your Child Survive Divorce*, p. 90.

69. Interview by author, Richfield, Minnesota, July 1999.

70. Telephone interview by author, July 1999.

71. Telephone interview by author, June 1999.

72. Quoted in Lansky, *Divorce Book for Parents*, p. 149.

73. Interview by author, Bloomington, Minnesota, September 1999.

74. Interview by author, Minneapolis, Minnesota, July 1999.

75. Interview by author, Minneapolis, Minnesota, July 1999.

76. Telephone interview by author, June 1999.

77. Telephone interview by author, June 1999.

78. Telephone interview by author, June 1999.

79. Interview by author, St. Paul, Minnesota, July 1999.

80. Interview by author, Minneapolis, Minnesota, June 1999.

81. Interview by author, Minneapolis, Minnesota, February 1999.

82. Interview by author, Minneapolis, Minnesota, July 1999.

83. Telephone interview by author, June 1999.

84. Interview by author, Minneapolis, Minnesota, July 1999.

85. Telephone interview by author, June 1999.

86. Telephone interview by author, July 1999.

Chapter 5: Trying to Move Ahead

87. Quoted in David Van Biema, "The Price of a Broken Home," *Time*, February 27, 1995, p. 53.

88. Quoted in "Tales of Kids and Divorce," *MacLean's*, August 17, 1998, p. 49.

89. Quoted in Van Biema, "The Price of a Broken Home," p. 53.

90. Quoted in Karl Zinmeister, "Divorce's Toll on Children," *Current*, February 1997, p. 31.

91. Interview by author, Minneapolis, Minnesota, June 1999.

92. Telephone interview by author, July 1999.

93. Interview by author, Minneapolis, Minnesota, July 1999.

94. Quoted in Rentmeester, "Splintered Families," p. 167.

95. Interview by author, Minneapolis, Minnesota, August 1999.

96. Rentmeester, "Splintered Families," pp. 166–67.

97. Quoted in Beth Levine, *Divorce: Young People Caught in the Middle*. Springfield, NJ: Enslow Publishers, 1995, p. 89.

98. Telephone interview by author, September 1999.

99. Telephone interview by author, July 1999.

100. Interview by author, Minneapolis, Minnesota, September 1999.

101. Quoted in Diane Guernsey, "For the Children's Sake," *Town and Country Monthly*, January 1998, p. 118.

102. Interview by author, St. Paul, Minnesota, June 1999.

103. Quoted in "Split Decisions," *People*, June 29, 1998, p. 93.

104. Zinmeister, "Divorce's Toll on Children," p. 33.

Organizations
to Contact

The following organizations provide information about various aspects of divorce.

Children's Rights Council (CRC)
220 I St. NE, Suite 401
Washington, DC 20002-4362

The CRC distributes books and pamphlets specializing in shared custody information for children and parents. It promotes strengthened families through education and advocacy and works to achieve divorce and custody reforms that are healthier and more beneficial to children.

Committee for Mother and Child Rights (CMCR)
210 Ole Orchard Dr.
Clear Brook, VA 22624

The CMCR serves mothers who have either lost custody of their children or are experiencing custody problems. The purpose of this organization is to help mothers and children going through the trauma of contested custody and to educate the public about injustices they face.

Fathers for Equal Rights (FER)
PO Box 010847
Miami, FL 33101

The FER is made up of parents and grandparents involved in divorce and custody disputes. It fights discrimination against and provides support for men in divorce cases and makes recommendations to legislatures and courts about discrimination issues.

Parents Without Partners
7910 Woodmont Ave., Suite 1000
Washington, DC 20014

This organization provides support for parents in various communities, helping them meet regularly to discuss problems and share ideas on how best to provide a good and stable home for their children.

Single Parent Resource Center (SPRC)
141 W. 28th St.
New York, NY 10001

The SPRC provides information and a referral service on many subjects of concern to single parents, including teen issues, and publishes a monthly newsletter.

Suggestions for Further Reading

Nancy O'Keefe Bolick, *How to Survive Your Parents' Divorce*. New York: Franklin Watts, 1994. Readable, with helpful advice from teens.

Jill Krementz, *How It Feels When Parents Divorce*. New York: Alfred A. Knopf, 1984. Very easy reading; the chapters dealing with teenagers are nicely done, with good photographs.

Paula McGuire, *Putting It Together: Teenagers Talk About Family Breakups*. New York: Delacorte Press, 1987. Excellent primary quotations from teens with firsthand experience in divorced families.

Isolina Ricci, *Mom's House, Dad's House*. New York: Macmillan, 1980.

Glenda Riley, *Divorce: An American Tradition*. New York: Oxford University Press, 1991. Although the focus is on the changes in divorce over the years, the book has an excellent section on children of divorce, as well as helpful statistics on the rising number of young people affected by divorce.

Barbara Dafoe Whitehead, *The Divorce Culture*. New York: Alfred A. Knopf, 1997. Scholarly look at the contributors to divorce in our culture; excellent section on literature and children.

Works Consulted

Joseph Adelson, "Splitting Up," *Commentary*, September 1996.

Genevieve Clapp, *Divorce and New Beginnings: An Authoritative Guide to Recovery and Growth, Solo Parenting, and Stepfamilies*. New York: John Wiley and Sons, 1992. Good sections on single parenting and communicating with older children about divorce.

Nancy Dreger, "Divorce and the American Family," *Current Health* 2, November 1996.

Linda Bird Francke, *Growing Up Divorced*. New York: Linden Press, 1983. Helpful section on money issues between parents and teenagers.

Melvin Goldzband, *Quality Time: Easing the Children Through Divorce*. New York: McGraw-Hill, 1985. Very clear explanation of the ways divorce litigation can traumatize children and teens, as well as a helpful chapter on proactive steps that children and teens must take during their parents' divorce.

Diane Guernsey, "For the Children's Sake," *Town and Country Monthly*, January 1998.

Vicki Lansky, *Vicki Lansky's Divorce Book for Parents: Helping Your Children Cope with Divorce and Its Aftermath*. New York: New American Library, 1989. Excellent section on custody and the courts.

John Leo, "Where Marriage Is a Scary Word," *U.S. News & World Report*, February 5, 1996.

Beth Levine, *Divorce: Young People Caught in the Middle*. Springfield, NJ: Enslow Publishers, 1995.

M. Gary Neuman, *Helping Your Kids Cope with Divorce the Sandcastles Way*. New York: Times Books, 1998.

Marlien Rentmeester, "Splintered Families," *Seventeen*, December 1997.

Mary Ann Shaw, *Helping Your Child Survive Divorce*. Secaucus, NJ: Birch Lane Press, 1997. Helpful sections on separation and visitation.

"Split Decisions," *People*, June 29, 1998.

"Tales of Kids and Divorce," *MacLean's*, August 17, 1998.

Edward Teyber, *Helping Children Cope with Divorce*. New York: Lexington Books, 1992. Invaluable chapter on parent cooperation and conflict.

David Van Biema, "The Price of a Broken Home," *Time*, February 27, 1995.

Judith Wallerstein and Sandra Blakeslee, *Second Chances: Men, Women, and Children a Decade After Divorce*. New York: Ticknor and Fields, 1989.

Anthony E. Wolf, *"Why Did You Have to Get a Divorce? And When Can I Get a Hamster?"* New York: Noonday Press, 1998. Very readable account of specific situations that come up with teens and divorcing parents. Good section on visitation.

Karl Zinmeister, "Divorce's Toll on Children," *Current*, February 1997.

Index

Picture Credits

Cover photo: © Esbin-Anderson/The Image Works
© Ron Chapple/FPG International, 21, 42, 60, 70
© Daemmrich/Uniphoto, 12, 78
© Mary Kate Denny/PhotoEdit, 38, 57, 73
© Tony Freeman/PhotoEdit, 27
© Spencer Grant/PhotoEdit, 36
© Jeff Greenberg/PhotoEdit, 25
© Richard Hutchings/Photo Researchers, Inc., 33
© John Lawlor/FPG International, 14
© Michael Newman/PhotoEdit, 31
© PhotoDisc, 17, 23, 67
© Catherine Smith/Impact Visuals, 76
© Arthur Tilley/FPG International, 55
© Uniphoto, 50
© Jim Whitmer/FPG International, 45
© David Young-Wolfe/PhotoEdit, 43, 48

About the Author

Gail B. Stewart is the author of more than eighty books for children and young adults. She lives in Minnesota, with her husband Carl and their sons Ted, Elliot, and Flynn. When she is not writing, she spends her time reading, walking, and watching her sons play soccer.